The Infinite game

irah nodles

Published by irah nodles, 2026.

THE INFINITE GAME

First edition. January 29, 2026.

ISBN: 979-8233743375

Written by irah nodles.

Chapter 1: The Hallucination of Reality

The greatest lie you have ever been told—a lie repeated in every classroom, textbook, and laboratory since you were a child—is that the world you see around you is real.

You are taught that you are a biological accident, a sophisticated ape clinging to a rock spinning through a universe of dead matter. You are taught that your brain, a lump of wet biological tissue, somehow generates the miracle of the mind. This is the foundational myth of the modern world: that Matter leads to Mind. But if you wish to understand the engine of history, you must first invert this lie. The truth is the exact opposite: Mind leads to Matter.

To understand why, we must look to the architect of modern thought, Immanuel Kant. Kant understood a terrifying truth: we never touch the world itself. We never see the noumena, the raw, vibrating energy of the universe as it truly exists. We are forever barred from it. Instead, our minds act as a filter. We take that infinite, chaotic energy and force it through the lenses of Time and Space—concepts that do not exist in the universe but only within our own mental architecture.

What results is the phenomena—the "things to us". The chair you sit on, the borders on a map, the money in your pocket—these are not objective realities. They are a user interface, a collective hallucination we project outward to navigate the void. Reality is not something we observe; reality is what we imagine it to be.

Our ancestors, the hunter-gatherers of the Ice Age, understood this physics better than we do. They did not need the "scientific method" because they possessed something far more powerful: the Religious Imagination. They understood that the universe is not dead space, but a conscious vibration—a "Monad" or collective mind. They knew that the human mind was not a hard drive for storing facts, but an antenna tuned to the frequencies of this universal consciousness.

This is why the ancients could build pyramids without computers and navigate the vast Pacific without GPS. They were not thinking; they were channeling. They understood that Imagination is the animating force of the universe. When a group of people collectively imagines a story—whether it is a god, a nation, or a currency—that story creates a psychic gravity. It organizes the chaotic energy of the population into a laser beam of will.

This brings us to the Universal Law of History: **Power = Mass × Energy × Coordination.**

In this formula, "Mass" is just people and resources. But "Energy" is mental motivation—the hunger, the belief, the spiritual drive. And "Coordination" is the ability to act as a single organism.

This explains the great paradox of history: why the weak consistently conquer the strong. Why do rich, massive empires with millions of soldiers fall to small, starving tribes from the borderlands?

The Empire has the Mass. It has the gold, the cities, and the technology. But it has lost the hallucination. The people no longer believe the story. They are listless, cynical, and disconnected—a "Rat Utopia" of satisfied consumers eating themselves alive.

The tribe from the borderland—the "Wolf Pack"—has almost no Mass. They are poor. They are starving. But they possess infinite Energy and absolute Coordination. Because they lack material resources, they are forced to rely on the only resource that matters: each other. They share a mythology that binds them into a "hive mind".

When the Wolf Pack meets the Empire, the result is mathematically inevitable. The Empire is a collection of individuals fighting for a paycheck; the Wolf Pack is a single spiritual entity fighting for survival. The hallucination of the Wolf Pack overrides the reality of the Empire.

History, then, is not a linear progression of technology. It is a cyclical game where those who can harness the Religious Imagination to create Coordination will always shatter those who rely solely on material Mass. To understand what comes next, we must stop looking at the material world and start looking at the stories we tell ourselves—because the story is the only thing that is real.

Chapter 2: The Algorithm of Myth

If the universe is a collective hallucination, as we established in the previous chapter, then we must ask the next logical question: What is the software running the simulation?

If you look at human history, you see a peculiar phenomenon. You see millions of people—strangers who have never met, who owe each other nothing—waking up at the same time, working for the same currency, fighting the same wars, and worshipping the same gods. They move with the synchronized precision of a flock of birds or a school of fish.

How is this possible? If you were to try to organize just ten of your friends to go to dinner, it would be a logistical nightmare of conflicting egos and schedules. Yet, history is the story of millions of people acting as one.

The answer lies in the most powerful technology ever invented by the human mind: The Myth.

In the modern world, we dismiss myths as fairy tales—stories about Zeus throwing lightning bolts or dragons guarding gold. We think we have outgrown them. But this is a fatal misunderstanding. A myth is not a lie. A myth is an operating system. It is the software installed into the collective subconscious of a population that allows for Unconscious Coordination.

To understand why this is the ultimate weapon of history, we must return to the Universal Law of Power:

Power = Mass × Energy × Coordination

Mass is simply the number of people. Energy is their motivation—their hunger, their belief. But Coordination is the multiplier. Coordination is weighted three times more heavily than mass. A mob of a thousand angry people (Mass) with high adrenaline (Energy) but zero coordination will always be defeated by a squad of one hundred disciplined soldiers who move as a single organism.

There are two ways to achieve coordination. The first is Conscious Coordination, or conspiracy. This is when people meet in a smoke-filled room to plot. But conspiracies are weak. They create friction. Egos get in the way. Someone always talks. It is impossible to scale a conspiracy because humans are naturally selfish and treacherous.

The second way, the superior way, is Subconscious Coordination. This is when you don't need to give orders because everyone already knows what to do. They are following a script that has been downloaded into their minds since birth.

This script is the Myth.

When a society shares a mythology, they achieve Synchronicity—the ability to possess a "hive mind". Think of a soccer team. The best teams don't need to talk to each other. They move intuitively. If one player moves left, the other knows instantly to move right to cover the space. They are telepathic because they are playing the same game, bound by the same rules, aiming for the same goal.

History, then, is not a battle of armies; it is a battle of stories. The winner is the one who writes the most compelling script.

Let us look at the dawn of civilization to see this algorithm in action. In ancient Mesopotamia, the elites faced a problem. They needed the free, roaming hunter-gatherers to settle down, dig irrigation ditches, and farm grain to feed the growing cities. But farming is terrible work. It is backbreaking, repetitive slavery compared to the freedom of the hills. How do you force a free man to become a serf? You cannot just use a whip; there are too many of them.

You use a story.

The Sumerians created a myth called the *Debate between Sheep and Grain*. In this story, the Sheep and the Grain argue before the gods about who is more valuable. The Grain wins the argument, and the gods decree that agriculture is the divine order of the universe.

This story wasn't entertainment. It was political propaganda encoded as theology. It told the population: "Your suffering in the fields is not slavery; it is your divine duty to the gods." By accepting the story, the population accepted the hierarchy. They self-organized into a labor force without the need for constant coercion.

We see this mechanism at its most potent in the concept of Eschatology—the study of the end of the world.

Eschatologies are the ultimate scripts. Whether it is the Zoroastrian battle between Light and Dark, the Christian Second Coming, or the Marxist Revolution, these narratives tell you three things: where you came from, why you are suffering, and where you are going. They provide a trajectory.

When a group of people believes they are actors in a divine script destined to bring about the end of history—whether by building the Third Temple in Jerusalem or establishing the Dictatorship of the Proletariat—they become an unstoppable force. They sacrifice themselves willingly. They possess "frictionless cooperation" because they believe they are characters in a play written by God.

This brings us to the terrifying truth of the modern world. You believe you are an individual making your own choices. You believe you chose your career, your clothes, your political opinions.

You did not.

You are acting out a script written by dead men. You are a character in a myth called "Liberal Meritocracy" or "Nationalism" or "Consumerism." You go to school not to learn, but to undergo a ritual initiation that installs the software of the Nation-State into your brain. You work a job you hate to buy things you don't need because you are running the "Capitalist" script that equates accumulation with salvation.

The people who rule the world—the elites, the "secret societies," the architects of reality—are simply the ones who know they are in a play. They are the directors. They understand that if you can change the story, you change the physical reality.

Napoleon knew this. He wasn't a great general because he was a better tactician; he was a great general because he cast himself as the

Messiah of the French Revolution, the Roman Emperor reborn. He created a myth of invincibility that energized his troops to march across Europe. He hacked the collective unconscious.

To understand the history that follows, you must learn to see the invisible lines of the script. You must stop looking at events as random occurrences and start seeing them as scenes in a grand drama.

The world is a stage. The question is: Are you the writer, the actor, or merely the prop?

Chapter 3: The Paradox of Resources

If you were to look at a map of the world at any major turning point in history—whether it is 1200 BC, 400 BC, or 1200 AD—and place a bet on who would conquer whom, you would almost certainly lose your money.

You would look at the map and see the Empire. It is vast, colored in solid imperial purple or red. It has the Mass. It has millions of subjects, towering stone cities, irrigation networks that defy nature, and vaults overflowing with gold. It has a standing army of professional soldiers equipped with the finest steel and armor.

Then you would look at the periphery, the "Borderlands." Here, there are no cities, only tents or mud huts. The people are few—perhaps one-hundredth the population of the Empire. They are poor, illiterate, and smell of their livestock. They have no gold, no bureaucracy, and often, no iron.

Any rational bookmaker would give the Empire odds of a thousand to one. And yet, time and time again, the history of the world is the story of the starving tribe from the mountains or the steppes descending upon the golden city and burning it to the ground. The Mongols conquered China; the Macedonians conquered Persia; the "Sea Peoples" dismantled the Bronze Age.

To understand why this happens—why the poor consistently conquer the rich—we must apply the Universal Law of History:

Power = Mass × Energy × Coordination

In this equation, the variables are not weighted equally. Mass (resources and population) is the least important factor. Energy (the will to fight/hunger) is weighted twice as heavily. But Coordination (unity/synchronicity) is weighted three times as heavily.

The Empire relies entirely on Mass. It mistakes bulk for strength. But the Borderland, precisely because it is poor, possesses infinite Energy and perfect Coordination. This chapter explains the physics of the "Wolf Pack" versus the "Fatted Calf."

The Trap of Abundance

Let us look first at the Empire. When a civilization succeeds, it falls into a trap of its own making. It creates Abundance.

In a wealthy society, the elites stop working. They become "rent-seekers," extracting wealth from the peasantry rather than creating new value. They become risk-averse. If you have a mansion, a position at court, and a vault of gold, you have everything to lose. You do not want to rock the boat; you want to maintain the status quo. This leads to Stagnation.

Worse, wealth destroys Coordination. In the Empire, people are strangers to one another. They are bound together not by blood or loyalty, but by money. When the Empire needs to fight a war, the citizens are too comfortable to fight. So, the Empire uses its Mass (wealth) to buy an army. They hire mercenaries—often the very barbarians from the borderlands they are trying to keep out.

A mercenary army has Mass, but it has zero Energy (devotion) and zero Coordination (love). They are fighting for a paycheck. If the battle turns against them, they run. If the money runs out, they turn on their masters.

The Wolf Pack: The Logic of the Borderlands

Now, look at the Borderland—the steppes of Mongolia, the mountains of Macedon, or the fjords of Scandinavia.

Here, geography is a cruel teacher. The land is poor. You cannot farm; you must herd or hunt. Resources are scarce. This scarcity forces a different kind of social physics.

First, it creates Energy. These people are hungry. They are desperate. They look at the Empire and see a life they cannot have unless they take it. They have "nothing to lose," which makes them capable of taking risks that a civilized man would consider insane.

Second, and most importantly, scarcity creates Coordination. In the steppe or the mountains, you cannot survive alone. If you are alone, you die. You must rely on your tribe. This creates a bond that the Arab historian Ibn Khaldun called *Asabiyyah*—a social cohesion so tight that the tribe acts as a single organism.

This dynamic finds its ultimate ancestor in the **Yamna** culture. Around 3300 BC, on the Pontic-Caspian steppe, a group of cattle herders did something that changed the human genome forever: they domesticated the horse and invented the war chariot. The Yamna were the original "Wolf Pack." They spread out from the steppe, their DNA overwriting the populations of Europe and South Asia. They provided the hardware of conquest—the mobile, coordinate strike force—and every conquering tribe that followed was merely echoing their innovation.

This is the Wolf Pack. A pack of wolves is smaller than a herd of buffalo, but the wolves win because they move with Synchronicity. They communicate without words. They trust that if they leap, their brother will be there to cover them.

The Engine of Conquest

This dynamic played out with terrifying clarity in the rise of Genghis Khan.

In the 13th century, the Mongols—spiritual successors to the Yamna—were a scattered collection of starving tribes living in yurts. They faced the Jin Dynasty of China and the Khwarazmian Empire of Persia—civilizations with millions of people, gunpowder, and walled cities.

By all traditional metrics, the Mongols should have been crushed. But the Mongols had the formula.

- **Mass:** Low.

- **Energy:** Infinite. They believed they were on a divine mission from the "Eternal Blue Sky" to conquer the earth.

They were driven by the "escalation dominance" of the desperate—if you punched them, they would burn your city to the ground.

- **Coordination:** Absolute. A Mongol warrior learned to ride and shoot before he could walk. They fought in units of ten. If one man in the unit ran away, all ten were executed. If one unit ran, the larger group of a hundred was executed. This created a psychological lattice where betrayal was impossible.

When the Mongol Wolf Pack hit the Chinese Empire, the Empire crumbled. The Chinese armies were massive, but they were composed of conscripted peasants led by corrupt bureaucrats who hated each other. One Mongol generated more force than a thousand conscripts because the Mongol was fighting for his life and his brothers, while the conscript was fighting for a tax collector.

The Oceanic Current of History

This reveals the secret mechanism of history: The Oceanic Current.

Civilizations do not exist in a vacuum. As an Empire expands, it trades with the Borderlands. It hires them as mercenaries. It buys their furs or their slaves. In doing so, the Empire inadvertently energizes the Borderland. It transfers wealth and technology to the very people who will eventually destroy it.

The Romans trained the Goths who sacked Rome. The Chinese trained the Mongols who conquered China. The British trained the American colonists who overthrew them.

History is a cycle of Creative Destruction. The rich become fat, lazy, and unconnected. They build walls to protect their hoard. But the poor, driven by the physics of the Universal Law, develop the Energy and Coordination to breach those walls.

The paradox of resources is that having them makes you weak, while needing them makes you strong. The rich have Mass, but the poor have History on their side.

Chapter 4: The Monotheistic Revolution

If the story of the Yamna was the hardware update of human history—introducing the physical tools of horses, wheels, and chariots—then what happened next was the ultimate software update. It was a psychological revolution so profound that it literally rewired the human brain, separating us from the natural world and placing us inside a simulation of our own making.

This was the invention of Monotheism.

To understand why this happened, we must look at the limits of the old world. In the polytheistic systems of the Greeks, Romans, and Mesopotamians, the world was a chaotic marketplace of deities. Each city had its god; each river had its spirit. When you went to war, your god fought their god. If you lost, it meant your god was weaker, so you bowed to the winner's deity.

This system worked for city-states. It respected the diversity of the human experience. But it had a fatal flaw: it could not scale. You cannot build a global empire on a foundation of a thousand bickering gods. If you want to rule the world, you cannot just have a stronger god; you need the *only* God.

The Council of Nicaea: The Architecture of Abstraction

The pivot point of this revolution was not the birth of Jesus, but a political meeting in 325 AD: the Council of Nicaea, convened by the Roman Emperor Constantine.

Constantine was a brilliant game theorist. He realized that the Roman Empire was fracturing because it lacked a unified operating system. He needed a religion that could bind millions of disparate people—Gauls, Greeks, Egyptians, Syrians—into a single obedient organism. He chose Christianity, but he had to engineer it first.

At Nicaea, the bishops engineered the concept of the Holy Trinity. They decreed that God was the Father, the Son, and the Holy Spirit—three distinct entities that were simultaneously one.

To the logical mind, this is nonsense. 1 + 1 + 1 cannot equal 1. But this logical impossibility was the feature, not the bug. By forcing the human mind to accept that three can be one, that God is both dead (Jesus on the cross) and eternal, the Church broke the human reliance on material reality. They trained the mind to accept Abstraction.

If you can believe in the Trinity, you can believe that a symbol is the reality. This cognitive leap gave birth to the three hallucinations that govern the modern world: Money, the Individual, and the Nation-State.

The First Hallucination: The Individual

In the ancient world—the world of the tribe and the polis—the "Individual" did not exist. You were a part of a whole. If you committed a crime, your community was punished. If you achieved glory, it belonged to your ancestors. The worst punishment was not death, but exile—to be cut off from the body of the tribe.

Monotheism inverted this. It created a direct line between the singular soul and the singular God. Salvation became a private matter. It no longer mattered what your community did; it mattered what you believed. This shattered the collective consciousness of the tribe and created the atomic Individual—a being defined not by their relationships, but by their internal faith.

This was a necessary innovation for empire. An empire cannot manage thousands of tribes with their own customs. But it can manage millions of individuals, each anxious about their own personal salvation, each striving to follow a universal law.

The Second Hallucination: The Nation-State

Once you have the concept of the "One True God," you can create the "One True State."

In the pagan world, a king was just a man favored by the gods. He could lose that favor tomorrow. But in the monotheistic worldview, the King is God's anointed representative. The State becomes a divine entity.

This allowed for the abstraction of the Nation-State. A nation is not a physical reality; you cannot touch "France" or "America." They are lines on a map and stories in our heads. But because the monotheistic mind had been trained to value the abstract over the material, people began to die for the "Nation" just as they would die for God.

The State became the new church. It demanded taxes (tithing), it demanded blood (sacrifice), and in return, it offered identity and salvation.

The Third Hallucination: Money

The most powerful abstraction of all, however, was Money.

Before this revolution, wealth was tangible: cows, grain, land. You could not fake it. But the logic of the Trinity—that a symbol (Jesus) represents the infinite (God)—laid the groundwork for modern capitalism.

Monotheism taught us that Nothing can be Everything. Just as the Eucharist turns bread into the body of Christ through faith, the state can turn paper into value through faith.

This is the secret history of capitalism. It is not an economic system; it is a religious system. It requires you to believe that a piece of paper, or a digit on a screen, holds the energy of the universe. When we transitioned from the Mother Goddess (who gave us abundance) to the Sky God (who demands tribute), we transitioned from a world of natural resources to a world of abstract debt.

The Great Separation

The cost of this revolution was our connection to reality.

In the animistic and polytheistic worlds, the divine was everywhere—in the trees, the rivers, the animals. We were part of a "Conscious Universe". Monotheism stripped the world of its spirit. It placed God in a distant heaven, leaving the earth as dead matter to be exploited.

We gained the power to organize billions of people. We gained the capacity for infinite economic growth through credit. We gained the modern self. But we lost the world. We trapped ourselves in a "symbolic reality" where we worship the shadows on the wall—money, status, borders—while the fire of the true universe burns unnoticed behind us.

The machine was now fully operational. The hardware of the Yamna and the software of Nicaea had combined. The stage was set for the Gunpowder Revolution and the final conquest of the globe.

Chapter 5: The Gunpowder Revolution and the Nation-State

If the invention of Monotheism was the software update that allowed humanity to scale, the invention of Gunpowder was the hardware update that forced us to submit.

For a thousand years, the game of power in Europe was played by a small elite: the Knights. A knight was a tank. Encased in expensive steel, mounted on a warhorse, and trained from childhood in the art of violence, a single knight could slaughter a hundred peasants without breaking a sweat. This reality created Feudalism. Because violence was expensive and required a lifetime of training, power was decentralized. The King was merely a figurehead; real power lay with the local lords who owned the land, the armor, and the time.

Then, chemistry killed the caste system.

When gunpowder arrived in Europe—ironically, imported from the East via the Pax Mongolica—it changed the physics of the game instantly. A musket ball, fired by a starving peasant with two weeks of training, could punch through the finest plate armor money could buy. Suddenly, the lifetime of training, the code of chivalry, and the expensive warhorse were obsolete. The Knight was dead.

This was not a liberation; it was a transition to a new, more terrifying form of slavery. This was the birth of the Gunpowder Revolution, and it demanded a new social architecture: the Nation-State.

The Logic of Mass and Coordination

To win a war with knights, you needed quality. To win a war with gunpowder, you needed Quantity and Coordination.

Gunpowder weapons in their infancy were inaccurate and slow. To be effective, you needed thousands of men standing in straight lines, firing in volleys at the exact same second. You needed Mass. But you also needed an industrial supply chain to mine the saltpeter, cast the cannons, and standardize the ammunition.

A local feudal lord could not afford this. Only a centralized state with the power to tax millions of people could build the foundries, supply the uniforms, and feed the armies. This necessity crushed the local lords and centralized power into the hands of the Monarch. The era of the "State" had begun.

But the State faced a new problem. How do you get a hundred thousand peasants to stand in a line and walk into cannon fire? You cannot force them all; there are too many of them. If they turn their muskets around, the King is dead.

You need a new software to run this hardware. You need Synchronicity.

The Invention of the School

We like to believe that public schools were invented to enlighten the population, to teach us literature and mathematics. This is a lie. Mass schooling was invented by the Prussian military state for one purpose: to create obedient soldiers and factory workers.

The Prussians, surrounded by enemies and lacking natural borders, realized that to survive, they needed to maximize Coordination. They needed a population that responded to orders like a single organism. They needed Synchronicity—the ability of a group to act with a hive mind.

The school system was designed to strip the individual of their autonomy. You wear a uniform. You stand in line. You move when the bell rings. You memorize facts without questioning them. You are graded on your ability to conform. This was the psychological conditioning required to create a "Whole Society" war machine. It transformed the chaotic, organic human being into a standardized brick in the wall of the State.

Societies that mastered Synchronicity—like Prussia (later Germany) and Japan—punched far above their weight. They became the "Hammer" in a world of anvils because they could channel the total energy of their population into a single vector of force.

The Social Contract: The Great Bribe

To complete the transformation, the State needed to replace the King with a new God. They needed a story that would make a man willing to die not for a person, but for an abstraction.

This abstraction was the Nation.

Before this era, people identified with their village or their religion. The concept of being "French" or "German" did not exist. The elites invented nationalism to solve the problem of Elite Overproduction and the need for mass conscription.

This birthed the Social Contract. The deal was simple: the State would grant you Rights—the right to vote, the right to own property, the right to call yourself a "Citizen"—and in exchange, you gave the State your life.

This culminated in the French Revolution. When the monarchies of Europe attacked France, the French did something unprecedented. They declared *levée en masse*—total mass conscription. They put guns in the hands of the people. The people did not revolt; they marched. They marched because they believed they were fighting for "France," for "Liberty," for themselves.

Napoleon Bonaparte was the first to fully harness this new energy. He didn't just have an army; he had a Nation. His soldiers moved faster, fought harder, and died more willingly than the mercenary armies of his enemies because they were powered by the religious energy of Nationalism.

The Divergence: Why the West Won

Here lies the answer to the great riddle of history: Why did the West conquer the world?

China invented gunpowder centuries before Europe. China had the bureaucracy, the population, and the wealth. By all metrics of Game Theory, China should have ruled the globe.

But China refused to change its software. The Confucian bureaucracy feared that if they armed the people and taught them to drill, the people might overthrow the bureaucracy. They chose internal stability over external power. They chose to suppress the technology to maintain the social hierarchy.

Europe had no such luxury. Europe was a "Warring States" ecosystem of constant, existential competition. If you did not adopt the Nation-State, if you did not build the schools, if you did not industrialize, you would be conquered by your neighbor who did.

The Gunpowder Revolution forced the West into a "Whole Society" approach to warfare. It fused the State, the Economy, and the Population into a single engine of conquest. The "Individual" was forged in the fires of this era—not as a free spirit, but as a component of the Machine.

The hardware was ready. The software was installed. Now, the Machine needed fuel. And that fuel would come from a new, abstract god that would soon eclipse the Nation itself: Capital.

Chapter 6: The Rise of Transnational Capital

If the Gunpowder Revolution created the body of the modern state—the standing armies, the bureaucracy, the disciplined masses—then the Financial Revolution created its blood.

For thousands of years, the definition of wealth was simple: land and gold. The Spanish Empire, the dominant power of the 16th century, operated on this old logic. They sailed to the New World, enslaved the population, and extracted literal mountains of silver and gold. They believed that whoever had the biggest pile of metal would win the game.

They were wrong. Spain went bankrupt multiple times while sitting on a throne of gold. Why? Because they failed to understand the new physics of power. They were defeated by a small, swampy, resource-poor nation that invented a weapon far more powerful than the galleon: Transnational Capital.

The Dutch Invention: Equity as Energy

The Dutch Republic had a problem. They were tiny, they were fighting the massive Spanish Empire, and they had no natural resources. To survive, they had to hack the game.

Their invention was the Dutch East India Company (VOC), founded in 1602. Before this, trade was a royal monopoly or a high-risk gamble for individuals. The Dutch changed the rules by inventing Equity. They allowed ordinary citizens to buy shares in the company.

This did something magical to the "Energy" variable in our Universal Law (**Power = Mass × Energy × Coordination**). By giving the population a financial stake in the success of the state's ventures, they aligned the incentives of the government, the merchants, and the common people. While Spanish sailors fought for a king who didn't know their names, Dutch sailors fought for their own dividends. The

Dutch discovered that a unified, incentivized population with a line of credit could outspend and outfight a king with a pile of gold.

The Merger: The Invasion of England

The Dutch system had one fatal flaw: geography. The Netherlands is flat and sits right next to the major land powers of Europe. No matter how much money they made, they were always at risk of invasion by the French or Spanish armies.

The Dutch elite realized they needed a fortress. They looked across the channel and saw England—an island protected by the sea, defensible and secure.

What history books call the "Glorious Revolution" of 1688 was not a democratic uprising; it was a corporate merger. The Dutch elite, led by William of Orange, effectively moved their headquarters from Amsterdam to London. They brought with them their financial technology, their stock market, and their concept of the merchant-state.

The Bank of England: The Global Safe Haven

Once established in London, this new Anglo-Dutch elite created the ultimate engine of war and control: the Bank of England, founded in 1694.

This was the birth of the modern world. The deal was simple but revolutionary: the Bank was a private corporation that would lend money to the King. The King would not pay back the principal; he would only pay the interest, using taxes collected from the people.

But there is a deeper function to this institution, one that explains the true mechanism of global power. The Bank of England became the world's first true "Safe Haven." It created a global system where elites from every nation—whether Indian Maharajas, Ottoman Pashas, or Chinese Mandarins—could steal from their own populations and store the wealth safely in London.

The British Empire was not just a conqueror; it was a service provider for the global corrupt. It told the ruling classes of the world: "Oppress your people, extract their wealth, and send it to us. We will protect it with our Navy and pay you interest on your own stolen gold."

This created a new form of government: the Transnational Oligarchy. In this system, the King and the Parliament are just managers; the real power lies with the private interests who control the ledger. It created a class of people who have no loyalty to any nation, only to the preservation of their capital.

The New God: Capital

By the 18th century, the transformation was complete. The "Divine Right of Kings" was dead, replaced by the "Divine Right of Capital." John Locke, the philosopher of this new order, argued that the government existed solely to protect Private Property.

It didn't matter how you got the property. You could have stolen it, enslaved people for it, or seized it in a war. Once it was yours, the state's only job was to protect it. This legalized piracy on a global scale.

The British Empire became the first true Transnational Corporation. It did not conquer land for the glory of God or the King; it conquered to open markets, enforce debt collection, and ensure the flow of interest payments back to the City of London.

The mechanism of control had shifted. You no longer needed to station soldiers in every village. If you controlled the debt, you owned the people. The chains of iron had been replaced by chains of gold, and the world had entered the age of Financialization. The machine was now hungry for the whole world.

Chapter 7: The Enlightenment Trap

By the 18th century, the old gods were dying. The Protestant Reformation had shattered the unity of the Church, and the Scientific Revolution had demystified the heavens. The European mind, stripped of its ancient superstitions, looked into the void and declared a new monarch: Reason.

We are taught that the Enlightenment was the liberation of humanity—the moment we grew up, cast aside our chains, and embraced science, democracy, and human rights. This is the "Whig interpretation of history," a fairy tale of linear progress.

Psychohistory reveals a darker truth. The Enlightenment did not liberate us; it merely changed management. By killing the "Divine," we did not become free. We became orphans. And to fill the terrifying silence left by God, we invented two new, materialistic deities that would enslave the modern world far more effectively than any pope or king: The Economy and The Self.

The architects of this new prison were two men who fundamentally rewrote the operating system of the human mind: Karl Marx and Sigmund Freud.

The Materialist Trap: Karl Marx

Karl Marx was a genius of diagnosis but a fool of prescription. He looked at the Industrial Revolution—the smoking factories of Manchester and the slums of London—and he saw the machine for what it was: a vampire.

Marx correctly identified the psychopathology of capitalism: Alienation. In the ancient world, a craftsman made a vase. He put his soul into it. When he gave it to someone, he wasn't just exchanging goods; he was exchanging a piece of his humanity. The object contained the "divine spark" of its creator.

Capitalism destroyed this. It replaced "use value" (what a thing does) with "exchange value" (what a thing costs). It turned the human being from a creator into a "hand"—a specialized cog in a machine, alienated from the product of his labor, alienated from nature, and alienated from his fellow man. Marx saw that money had become a new god, a force that turned everything sacred into a commodity.

But Marx's solution was a trap. He believed that the problem was Private Property. He argued that if we just seized the means of production and gave them to the state (the Vanguard), we would enter a worker's paradise.

Marx failed because he was a materialist. He believed that economics drove history. But as we have established, Religion drives history. Humans do not just want bread; they want Status and Meaning. They want to feel superior to their neighbor. They want to connect with the infinite.

By removing God and replacing Him with the State, Marx didn't create freedom. He created a Theocracy without God. Communism became just another religion, with its own prophets (Lenin/Mao), its own scriptures (Das Kapital), and its own Inquisition (the KGB). It was the same "Empire" software running on different hardware.

The Psychological Trap: Sigmund Freud

While Marx was enslaving man to the State, Sigmund Freud was enslaving man to the Self.

The official history of psychology tells us that Freud was a courageous scientist who discovered the "Unconscious." The secret history is that Freud was a master propagandist who helped the elite weaponize guilt.

In the late 19th century, Freud began treating "hysterical" women in Vienna. These women suffered from paralysis, anxiety, and depression. Under hypnosis, they told Freud a terrible truth: they had been sexually abused by their fathers, uncles, and the pillars of Viennese high society.

Freud initially believed them. He called it the "Seduction Theory." He was on the verge of exposing the dark, predatory underbelly of the European elite.

But then, Freud realized the cost. If he published this truth, the elite would destroy him. He would lose his funding, his status, and perhaps his life. So, Freud committed the ultimate intellectual betrayal. He flipped the script.

He invented the Oedipus Complex. He told the world that these women were not victims of abuse; they were victims of their own fantasies. He claimed that children wanted to sleep with their parents, and their hysteria was the result of repressing these dark, internal desires.

This was the birth of Gaslighting as a science.

Freud shifted the blame from the perpetrator (the elite) to the victim (the individual). He convinced humanity that the source of our misery was not the external world—not the unjust society, the war-mongering state, or the predatory capitalist—but our own broken, dirty subconscious.

The Cult of the Self

The fusion of these ideas created the Modern Trap.

From Marx, we learned to view everything through the lens of material gain. From Freud (and his nephew, Edward Bernays), the elites learned that humans are not rational actors, but bundles of insecurity and desire that can be manipulated.

This birthed the Consumer.

Before the 20th century, people defined themselves by their community, their faith, and their duties. The Enlightenment destroyed these bonds. It left the individual naked and alone, terrified of the silence.

To quell this anxiety, the system offered a new drug: The Cult of the Self. We were taught that the goal of life is not *Eudaimonia* (flourishing/virtue) but Happiness (pleasure/comfort). We were taught to look inward, to "find ourselves," to obsess over our own psychology.

This is the ultimate mechanism of control. If you are obsessed with your own anxiety, your own identity, and your own material accumulation, you cannot form the Cohesion necessary to fight the power structure. You become a "Psychological Man"—a creature who goes to therapy to cope with a sick society rather than rising up to change it.

We traded the "Divine Spark" for a dopamine hit. We traded the infinite imagination of the Monad for the shallow screen of the smartphone. The Enlightenment promised to make us gods; instead, it turned us into rats in a cage, pressing a lever for a pellet, dreaming we are free.

Chapter 8: The Game of Empires

By the dawn of the 20th century, the board was set. The era of small kings and localized conflicts was over. The industrial revolution had scaled the game of power to a planetary level, and the world was now divided between three great civilizational "souls," each vying for total domination. These were not just nations; they were competing operating systems for the human species.

To understand the bloodbath of the 20th century, we must look past the dates and battles and analyze the Psychohistory of the combatants: the Anglo-American, the German, and the Russian.

The Three Souls

First, there was the Anglo-American Soul. Geography is destiny, and because Britain and America are protected by water—one an island, the other a continental fortress—their soul is Utilitarian and Empirical. They are not interested in "Truth" with a capital T; they are interested in "what works". Their philosophy, born of John Locke and Jeremy Bentham, views society as a marketplace of individuals pursuing life, liberty, and property. It is a soul of commerce, optimism, and narrow, practical logic.

Opposing them was the German Soul. Situated in the center of Europe, surrounded by enemies, the Germans could not afford the luxury of individualism. Their soul is defined by Idealism and the Will to Power (*Wille zur Macht*). Drawing on philosophers like Hegel and Nietzsche, the German mind believes that reality is not something you observe, but something you impose through the strength of your will. They sought Synchronicity—the ability of a population to move, think, and fight as a single, terrifying organism.

Finally, there was the Russian Soul. Vast, cold, and undefendable, Russia is a land of tragedy. The Russian soul is Fatalistic and Mystical. They do not believe in the pursuit of happiness; they believe in the necessity of suffering. Their imagination is "dark" and "broad," capable of enduring pain that would shatter a Westerner.

The history of the 20th century is the story of the German "Will" crashing against the Russian "Endurance," while the Anglo-American "Banker" watched from the sidelines, waiting to collect the winnings.

The German Move: The Ubermensch

The German game began with a realization: they were trapped. The British Empire controlled the seas, choking Germany's access to resources. To survive, Germany needed *Lebensraum* (living space) in the East.

To achieve this, the German elite—the Army and the Secret Societies—needed a figurehead who could magnetize the population into total synchronicity. They needed an Ubermensch (Superman), a concept taken from Nietzsche to describe a man who can step outside of history and warp reality to his will.

Enter Adolf Hitler. History tells us he seized power; game theory suggests he was cast for a role. He was an intelligence agent for the Army, sent to infiltrate the worker's parties. He was an actor who auditioned for the role of the Messiah, promising to restore the shattered pride of the German people through the sheer force of will. The Nazis were not a political party; they were a religious cult dedicated to the defiance of reality through movement and expansion.

The Russian Counter-Move: The Man of Steel

Facing the German onslaught was a man who remains the greatest riddle of the modern age: Joseph Stalin.

Western historians portray Stalin as a paranoid brute. Psychohistory reveals him as a supreme Game Theorist. Stalin was not a pampered intellectual like Lenin or Trotsky; he was a creature of the shadows—a bank robber, a gangster, and a police informant. He understood that in a world of sharks, you do not survive by being smart; you survive by being ruthless.

Stalin prepared for the inevitable war not by building more tanks, but by hacking his own society. The Great Purge of the 1930s, where he killed his own generals, was not merely madness. It was a calculated "creative destruction." By eliminating the old, conservative leadership, he forced the Red Army to become young, flexible, and innovative. He terrorized his own population into a state of total war capability before the first shot was fired.

The Game of 1941

This leads us to the most misunderstood event in history: Operation Barbarossa, the German invasion of Russia in 1941.

Conventional history claims Stalin was a fool who trusted Hitler. Game theory asks: What was the only way for the Soviet Union to win?

Let us run the scenarios:

1. **Scenario A:** Stalin attacks Germany. The West (Britain/America) immediately joins Germany to crush the spread of Communism. Russia loses.
2. **Scenario B:** Germany attacks Russia and gets stuck at the border. The West watches them destroy each other. Russia eventually collapses from lack of resources.
3. **Scenario C (The Winning Move):** Germany attacks, breaks through, and threatens to swallow Russia whole.

Only in Scenario C does the Anglo-American Empire panic. If Germany takes Russia's resources, Germany becomes invincible. Therefore, the Americans are forced to save Stalin. They send Lend-Lease aid—$250 billion in today's money—industrializing the Soviet Union for free.

Stalin played the ultimate gambit. He had to look weak. He had to lure the German wolf deep into the Russian snow. He tricked Hitler by uttering the three words a predator loves to hear: "I trust you". He played the role of the sheep so convincingly that Hitler overextended his empire into oblivion.

The Victory of the "Third Player"

The war was a meat grinder. The Germans had the Will (Energy), but the Russians had the Mass and the Coordination born of existential terror. Stalin sacrificed 27 million of his own people to win the game.

But as the German and Russian souls tore each other apart, the third player made its move. The American Empire emerged from the ashes not as a combatant, but as the banker. While Europe burned, America built the factories. While the Old World destroyed its wealth, America accumulated it.

By 1945, the "Game of Empires" had a clear winner. The German soul was broken. The Russian soul was exhausted. The Anglo-American soul, having paid the lowest price in blood, purchased the world with the dollar. The stage was set for the final act of the modern era: Pax Americana.

Chapter 9: Pax Americana and the Meritocracy

In July 1944, while the embers of the Second World War still glowed across Europe and the Pacific, a different kind of conquest was taking place in the quiet mountains of New Hampshire. At the Mount Washington Hotel in Bretton Woods, delegates from forty-four nations gathered to design the operating system of the post-war world. They believed they were building a framework for peace. In reality, they were constructing the greatest empire in human history: Pax Americana.

The deal struck at Bretton Woods was elegant and ruthless. The United States, the only industrial power left standing, offered a seductively simple proposition: the US dollar would be the reserve currency of the world, pegged to gold. In exchange, the American Navy would patrol the oceans, guaranteeing free trade for everyone.

This was the "Exorbitant Privilege." It gave the United States the power of alchemy—the ability to print paper and have the world treat it as gold. It allowed America to export its inflation and import the world's resources. But to run an empire of this magnitude, America needed a new class of rulers. The old aristocracy—the drinking clubs of the WASP elite—were too lazy and too stupid to manage a global machine.

To maintain hegemony, the American Empire had to invent a new social technology: The Meritocracy.

The Sorting Hat: Industrializing the Elite

The architect of this new system was James Bryant Conant, the president of Harvard. He looked at his university—then a finishing school for the idle rich—and realized it was unfit for the atomic age. He partnered with Henry Chauncey to create a mechanism that would scientifically identify the most useful minds in the population and extract them for the service of the state.

They repurposed an IQ test used by the military and called it the SAT.

The narrative sold to the public was one of fairness: a poor farm boy from Kansas could score high, go to Harvard, and rule the world. It was the "American Dream" weaponized. But in practice, the Meritocracy became a "Venture Capital" firm for human souls. The elite universities stopped looking for scholars and started looking for "leaders"—high-risk, high-reward assets who would expand the empire's power.

This system fundamentally rewired the human experience. It transformed childhood from a time of exploration into a "Hunger Games" of endless competition. To succeed, a child had to be programmed from birth: perfect grades, perfect extracurriculars, perfect compliance. The family unit was repurposed into a factory for producing resume-padding achievers.

The Psychopathology of Power

Psychohistory asks: what kind of human being does this system produce?

The Meritocracy selects for a specific psychological profile: Dissociative Personality Disorder. To survive the grueling competition of the modern elite education system, the individual must learn to sever their connection to their own feelings. They must suppress their "true self"—the part that wants to play, love, and explore—and cultivate a "false self" that is obsessed with external validation and achievement.

We see the archetype in the "Golden Boy": the Navy SEAL turned Harvard doctor turned astronaut. Society calls this excellence; psychohistory calls it trauma response. These are not happy people. They are high-functioning, insecure overachievers who are terrified of failure. They are "specialists without spirit," running a machine they do not understand for a purpose they do not believe in.

This created an elite class that is technically brilliant but spiritually hollow. They possess high IQs but zero wisdom. They can manage a hedge fund or a drone war with algorithmic precision, but they lack the empathy and imagination required to sustain a civilization. They are the "managers" who replaced the "owners," and like all renters, they have no incentive to maintain the property—only to extract value from it before moving on.

Rat Utopia: The Terminal Phase

As the 20th century closed, the American Empire achieved total dominance. There were no more enemies to fight, no more frontiers to conquer. The West entered a state of unprecedented abundance.

This brings us to the terrifying experiments of John B. Calhoun and the concept of "Rat Utopia."

In the 1960s, Calhoun placed rats in a perfect environment with unlimited food, water, and no predators. He expected them to thrive. Instead, they went insane. As the population peaked, the social fabric disintegrated. The rats stopped breeding. They became hyper-aggressive or catatonic. A class of male rats, dubbed the "Beautiful Ones," withdrew from society entirely, spending their days grooming themselves and refusing to mate or fight.

Calhoun discovered a grim biological law: When a social animal has all its material needs met but has no role to play, it destroys itself.

The Meritocracy has turned the West into a human Rat Utopia. We have solved the problem of scarcity, but we have created a crisis of Status. Status is a zero-sum game. In a world of abundance, the competition for the few remaining seats of power becomes vicious and all-consuming.

We see the "Beautiful Ones" in the modern phenomenon of "Lying Flat" or "Quiet Quitting"—young people who realize the game is rigged and refuse to play. We see the breakdown of social cohesion as the "Elite Overproduction" leads to vicious factionalism, where the rich devour the rich.

The "American Game"—the belief that if you follow the rules, you will win—has broken. The empire is no longer a republic of citizens; it is a casino where the house has rigged the wheels. The population, sensing the fraud, has begun to check out, signaling the end of the mandate of heaven. The machine is still running, printing money and degrees, but the soul of the civilization has fled. The stage is set for the collapse.

Chapter 10: The Universal Law of Collapse

If you look at the timeline of every great civilization—from Rome to the Maya to the Han Dynasty—you see the same heartbeat. It is a biological rhythm that no amount of technology or money can suppress. Civilizations are not static structures; they are living organisms. They are born, they mature, they grow old, and they die.

This is the Universal Law of Collapse.

To understand where we are today, we must abandon the modern delusion of linear progress—the idea that things will just keep getting better forever because we have iPhones and democracy. Instead, we must look to the German philosopher Oswald Spengler, who argued that civilizations have a "life cycle". We must also look to the data of Peter Turchin, who mathematically modeled how societies destroy themselves through their own success.

The life cycle of a civilization consists of three distinct phases: Rise, Decline, and Collapse. We can measure the health of a society in any of these phases using three metrics: Energy (how hard people work), Openness (how much social mobility exists), and Cohesion (how much people trust each other).

The Anatomy of the Cycle

1. **The Rise: The Age of Consent**
   In the beginning, a civilization is poor but energetic. The leadership is open to talent because they have to be—if they aren't, the tribe dies. The society operates on Consent. People work together because they share a common vision and a common enemy. There is high social mobility; a peasant can become a general if he is good enough. This is the era of the "Wolf Pack"—high cohesion, high energy.
2. **The Decline: The Age of Deception**

Success breeds the virus of decline. As the society becomes wealthy, the elites stop leading and start hoarding. They want to pass their power to their children, not to the most talented. The system shifts from meritocracy to Oligarchy. To maintain their power without providing value, the elites turn to Deception. They gaslight the population. They tell you that the economy is booming when your wages are stagnant. They tell you that diversity is strength when social trust is fracturing. The bureaucracy expands to manage the decline, replacing innovation with paperwork and regulation. The goal is no longer growth; the goal is Stability—keeping the corpse warm.

3. **The Collapse: The Age of Coercion**
   Finally, the lies stop working. The money runs out. The social contract breaks. The elites can no longer bribe the people or trick them, so they must force them. This is the transition to Coercion. The state becomes authoritarian not out of strength, but out of weakness. It uses the police and the military to enforce what culture no longer can. This phase is sudden, violent, and inevitable.

The Symptoms of the End

We are currently living in the terminal phase of the Decline, teetering on the edge of Collapse. The signs are everywhere, visible through the lens of psychohistory.

1. **Death by Gerontocracy**
   The most defining characteristic of the modern West is that the old refuse to die. We live in a Gerontocracy—rule by the elderly. In a healthy society, the old step aside to let the young lead and innovate. In our society, the old hoard everything. They hold the real estate, the stocks, and the political offices. They have rigged the economy to protect their assets (inflation, housing bubbles) at the expense of the young, who are buried

in debt. The result is a psychological breakage. Young people look at the "game"—work hard, buy a house, have a family—and realize the math doesn't work. So they stop playing. They "Lie Flat" (Tang Ping). They quit. A society where the young refuse to struggle is a society that has no future.

2. **Elite Overproduction**
   Paradoxically, our society is destroying itself not because we lack elites, but because we have too many. This is Peter Turchin's theory of Elite Overproduction. We pump out millions of university graduates, telling them they are special, that they will be managers and leaders. But the number of power positions remains fixed. This creates a "Game of Musical Chairs" where ten people are fighting for one seat. The result is vicious factionalism. The elites turn on each other. They weaponize "cancel culture" and political polarization to destroy their rivals because the competition for status has become a zero-sum game of survival.
3. **The Financialization Trap**
   When a civilization is rising, the economy creates things (manufacturing). When a civilization is collapsing, the economy creates money (finance). We have entered the stage of Financialization, where capital grows faster than the real economy. The elites have stopped building factories and started building algorithms to extract rent. The stock market hits record highs while the infrastructure crumbles. It is a "Ponzi scheme" of debt that requires constant expansion to keep from imploding.
4. **The Immigration Trap**
   To prop up this dying system, the elites have pulled the final lever: Mass Immigration. They need bodies. They need immigrants to work the low-wage jobs that natives refuse to do,

and they need new consumers to keep the housing bubble inflated and the pension systems solvent. But while this fixes the economic numbers, it destroys the social numbers. It erodes Cohesion. A nation is not a hotel; it is a family. When you flood a society with strangers who share no common history or myth, you destroy the "hive mind" necessary to survive a crisis. You create a tower of Babel, ungovernable and mutually hostile.

The Rat Utopia

Ultimately, we are living through the grim reality of John B. Calhoun's "Rat Utopia." In his experiments, Calhoun gave rats unlimited food and no predators. He expected them to flourish. Instead, they stopped breeding. They became autistic, hyper-aggressive, or completely passive. The "Beautiful Ones" sat in the corners, grooming themselves, refusing to participate in society.

The West has become a Rat Utopia. We have solved the problem of survival, but we have lost the struggle that gives life meaning. We have become "specialists without spirit, sensualists without heart". The collapse that is coming is not just an economic correction; it is a biological reset. The old wood must burn so that the forest can grow again. The cycle cannot be stopped; it can only be endured.

Chapter 11: World War III and the Game Reset

We have now arrived at the precipice. If Psychohistory is the science of prediction, then we must look at the variables on the board today—the debt, the demographics, the spiritual exhaustion of the West—and follow the trajectory to its logical, mathematical conclusion. The conclusion is War.

In Game Theory, there is a concept known as the "Game Reset." When a game of Monopoly has gone on too long, when one player holds all the money and everyone else is bankrupt, the game stops being fun. The losers become restless. They threaten to flip the board. To prevent a revolution that destroys the players, the Game Masters must destroy the board themselves. They must burn the capital to save the system. This is the function of World War III.

The Trap of the Petrodollar

To understand why this war is inevitable, we must look at the engine of the American Empire: the US Dollar.

Since 1971, the dollar has not been backed by gold, but by oil and violence. The deal is simple: Saudi Arabia sells oil only in dollars, creating global demand for American currency. In exchange, the American military protects the Saudi regime. This allows America to print infinite money, exporting its inflation to the rest of the world.

But this system relies on one psychological pillar: the perception of American Invincibility. If the world believes the US military is a "paper tiger"—if it sees the US fail in Afghanistan or struggle in Ukraine—then the world stops fearing America. They stop buying dollars. The debt bomb explodes, and the American standard of living collapses overnight.

This brings us to Iran.

According to Game Theory, the American Empire must invade Iran. It is not a choice; it is a structural necessity. To restore faith in the dollar,

America must demonstrate "escalation dominance." It must seize the oil and the trade routes of the Middle East to force China and the world back into submission.

But this is a trap. The invasion of Iran is the "Sunk Cost Fallacy" weaponized on a geopolitical scale. Iran has mastered Asymmetrical Warfare. They will not fight the US Navy ship-for-ship; they will use cheap drones and missiles to swarm billion-dollar aircraft carriers. The US will send 100,000 troops, get bogged down, and be unable to leave without admitting defeat. This quagmire will drain the last of America's treasury and ignite the civil conflict already brewing at home.

The Hidden Script: Eschatology

However, to view this war solely through the lens of oil and money is to miss the deeper, darker operating system of history. We must return to the concept that Eschatology drives Geopolitics.

The elites who run the world—the "Secret Societies," the intelligence agencies, the religious fundamentalists—are not secular rationalists. They are following a script. They believe they are actors in a divine drama destined to bring about the End of Days.

There are three major eschatologies converging on the Middle East, acting as "unconscious coordination" mechanisms for World War III:

1. **Christian Zionism:** This group, which holds immense power in the US military and political system, believes in Premillennial Dispensationalism. Based on the writings of Isaac Newton and the Scofield Bible, they believe that for Jesus to return, the Jews must return to Israel, the Al-Aqsa Mosque must be destroyed, the Third Temple must be built, and the war of Gog and Magog must be fought. They want war because they want the Rapture.
2. **Jewish Messianism:** Hardline Zionists believe they must conquer "Greater Israel" and destroy their enemies to usher in the Messianic Age, where Israel becomes the light of the

nations and the center of the world. They are using the Christian Zionists as a "golem"—a tool to destroy Israel's enemies (Iran), knowing that once the war is won, the Christians can be discarded.

3. **The Katechon (Russia):** Vladimir Putin views himself not merely as a president, but as the Katechon—the biblical "Restrainer" who holds back the Antichrist. In the Orthodox worldview, the "Antichrist" is Western Liberalism—the civilization of the "Lie" that destroys gender, tradition, and spirit. Putin is fighting a metaphysical war to destroy the American Empire and restore the spiritual "Third Rome".

The Prediction: The Collapse of Pax Americana

When we feed these variables into our Psychohistory model, the future resolves into a terrifying clarity.

The United States will engage Iran. It will be a disaster. The internal contradictions of the American society—the Elite Overproduction, the Death by Gerontocracy, the racial and political polarization—will snap. The war abroad will trigger a Second American Civil War at home. The American Empire, bankrupt and broken, will be forced to retreat from the world stage, withdrawing to the Western Hemisphere.

This leaves a vacuum. Who fills it?

Pax Judaica: The New Rome

As the American Empire recedes, a new order will emerge from the ashes of the Middle East. It will not be a Chinese global hegemony, nor a Russian one. It will be Pax Judaica.

When the US military retreats, its infrastructure in the Middle East (CENTCOM) does not disappear; it is absorbed by the regional hegemon: Israel. Having destroyed its neighbors with American blood and treasure, Israel will stand alone as the technologically superior superpower of the region.

This new order will not be based on manufacturing or oil, but on the new gods of the 21st century: Technology, Intelligence, and Finance. We are already seeing the capital of the world shift. The Silicon Valley elite, the transnational hedge funds, and the surveillance technology sector are aligning with Tel Aviv and Jerusalem.

This fits the final pattern of the "Game." The vision of a world government centered in Jerusalem, ruled not by a king but by an all-seeing artificial intelligence (the "Mark of the Beast"), serves as the ultimate mechanism of control.

We are moving from the age of the Nation-State back to the age of the God-King—but this time, the God is a digital mind hosted in the Third Temple, and the control grid is total.

The cycle of history is closing. The "Garden of Eden" is being rebuilt, but it is a digital prison. The only way to escape the trap of the coming "Game Reset" is to realize that the game itself is a lie—to reject the script of the apocalypse and reclaim the Religious Imagination to write a new ending. But the window is closing fast. The pieces are already moving. The war has already begun.

Conclusion: Reclaiming the Imagination

We have reached the end of the labyrinth. We have traced the arc of history from the first hallucinations of the Ice Age shamans to the algorithmic tyranny of the modern surveillance state. We have seen how the Yamna invented the war machine, how Rome perfected the politics of trauma, and how the Bank of England turned debt into a god. We have analyzed the cold, mathematical laws of Psychohistory—Mass × Energy × Coordination—and seen how elites have used these laws to trap humanity in a cycle of rise, decline, and collapse.

But if you close this book believing that history is a prison from which there is no escape, then you have missed the final, most terrifying secret of the world.

The secret is this: **The prison is not locked.**

The ultimate mechanism of control used by the elites—from the Pharaohs of Egypt to the technocrats of Silicon Valley—is not armies, nor debt, nor surveillance. It is the suppression of the Human Imagination. They maintain power by convincing you that the material world is the only reality. They teach you that you are a biological accident, a "meat robot" driven by chemical impulses, living in a universe of dead matter. They teach you that the future is inevitable, that war is human nature, and that you are powerless against the systems of capital and the state.

This is the "Great Lie".

As we established in the beginning, drawing on Immanuel Kant and quantum mechanics, we do not live in an objective reality. We live in a Phenomenal World—a reality constructed by our minds filtering energy through time and space. This means that the world around us—the borders, the money, the hierarchies—is a collective hallucination. It only exists because we agree to imagine it together.

The elites understand this physics. They know that Mind leads to Matter. They know that if they can control the collective imagination through trauma, propaganda, and "spells" (narratives), they can warp physical reality to their will. They act as the "Game Masters," writing a script that the rest of us unconsciously act out.

But this physics applies to you, too.

The Physics of Love and Creation

To break the cycle of history—to escape the coming "Game Reset" of World War III—we must reclaim the two forces that truly govern the universe. These are not sentimental concepts; they are the fundamental physics of the Monad, the divine source of all being.

The first force is Love. In the game of empire, love is a weakness. It creates vulnerability. But in the true physics of the universe, Love is the Unifying Force. It is the gravity that holds the spiritual universe together. When Dante ascended to Paradise, he realized that the universe is not a cold void, but a web of connection bound by "the Love that moves the sun and the other stars". Love breaks the "Prisoner's Dilemma" of game theory because it dissolves the ego. It allows us to act not for self-interest, but for the whole, creating a "Superorganism" that is invincible.

The second force is Imagination. Imagination is the Animating Force. The universe desires to know itself, and it does so through us. We are the eyes and ears of the Monad. When we imagine a new possibility—when we write a poem, build a temple, or conceive of a just society—we are not just "thinking"; we are channeling the divine energy to create new worlds. The elites want you to be a "Consumer"—passive, dull, and reactive. The universe wants you to be a Creator.

The Choice: The Machine or the Garden

We stand now at a crossroads.

One path leads to the Machine. This is the path of Transhumanism, the final project of the current elite. It is the attempt to merge man with machine, to upload consciousness into a digital cloud, and to achieve immortality without a soul. It is the ultimate "Tower of Babel"—a sterile, controlled, eternal prison where the human heart is extinguished, and we become perfect, unfeeling gears in a system of total control.

The other path leads back to the Garden. This is the path of the Religious Imagination. It is the realization that we are co-creators with the divine. It requires us to reject the "Rat Utopia" of comfort and safety. It asks us to embrace the struggle, the pain, and the beauty of being human. It asks us to stop being "NPCs" (Non-Playable Characters) in someone else's script and to become the protagonists of our own.

The future is not written. The "Prophecies" of the end times—the war of Gog and Magog, the clash of civilizations—are just scripts written by madmen who want to force the end of history. We do not have to play their game.

If we can reclaim our imagination, if we can learn to love with the ferocity of Achilles weeping for Priam, and if we can coordinate through shared vision rather than shared fear, we can write a new ending.

The architecture of reality is not made of stone or steel. It is made of mind. The walls are only as strong as your belief in them.

Wake up. The dream is yours to dream.

About the Author

Irah nodles is pen name for a computer scientist and engineer specializing in game theory and psychohistory.

www.ingramcontent.com/pod-product-compliance
Ingram Content Group UK Ltd.
Pitfield, Milton Keynes, MK11 3LW, UK
UKHW041141300926
15471UKWH00011B/38

9 798233 743375